ARTHUR RACKHAM IN EAST ANGLIA

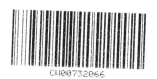

The young Arthur Rackham:
carte-de-visite photograph by Brixton photographers Treble & Son

ARTHUR RACKHAM IN EAST ANGLIA

FORTY OF HIS PEN & INK DRAWINGS

WITH AN INTRODUCTION BY
ALISON BARNES

POPPYLAND
PUBLISHING

ISBN 0 946148 73 2

Published by Poppyland Publishing, Cromer, NR27 9AN

Designed and set in 11½ on 15 pt Golden Cockerel by Watermark, Cromer, NR27 9AL.

Printed by Printing Services (Norwich) Ltd

ACKNOWLEDGEMENTS

NUMEROUS people have helped me with my research for this book and I am extremely grateful to them all, but I should like to thank in particular Mr David Clarke, Dr Philip Errington of Sotheby's Book Department, Mr David Ferrow, Mr Ron Fiske, Mr John Freeman of Tombland Books, Norwich, Mr Charles Harrison Wallace, Ms Caroline Jarrold and Ms Sarah Letts of Jarrold and Sons, Mr Christopher Smith of the Norfolk Heritage Centre, Norwich, Mr Richard Shackle and Ms Janc Stanway of Colchester Library, the staffs of Bloomsbury Book Auctions, the British Library, the Butler Library, Columbia University, New York, Cambridge City Library, Cambridge University Library, Castle Books, Colchester, Chelmsford Library, the Essex Record Office, the Guildhall Library, London, the Norfolk Record Office, Southend Library, the Suffolk Record Office, and the Victoria and Albert Museum, London.

I should also especially like to thank Ms Vivian Peto, Arthur Rackham's grand-daughter, for answering questions about him and allowing me to use his drawings in *Sunrise-Land*, and Ms Anne-

Stevenson Hobbs (Mrs Anne Wright), Rackham's great-niece, for providing me with many details of Rackham family history and letting me reproduce the hitherto unpublished photograph of the artist that appears here as frontispiece.

Acknowledgement is further made to Mr David Clarke for permitting the use of the unpublished Rackham caricature which features in the Introduction, to the Syndics of Cambridge University Library for allowing the Rackham sketch of Annie Berlyn and Mr Blake in their copy of Jarrold's *Guide to Wells* to appear in the Introduction, and to Colchester Library for providing six of the Rackham drawings reproduced in this book.

To Yolande, Gilles, Christophe, Patricia and Agnes with love

CONTENTS

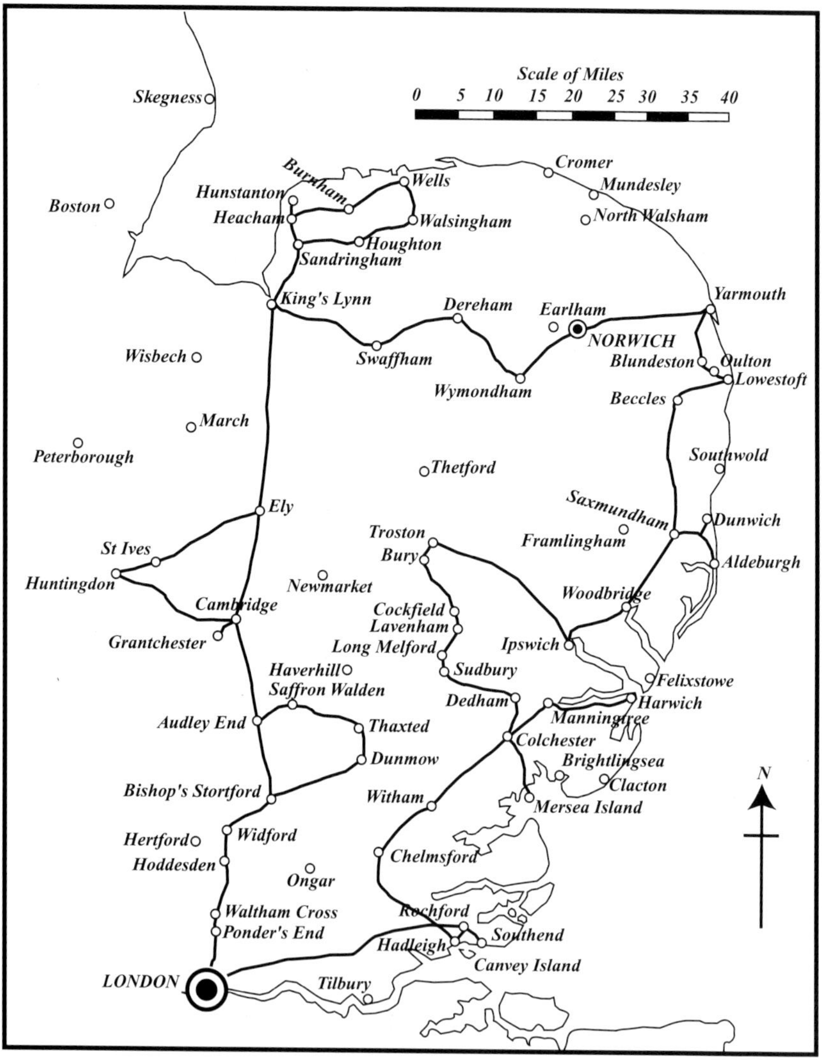

A map of East Anglia showing all the places visited by Rackham and his colleagues. Based on a sketch map of 1923, the map shows railway lines operating in Rackham's day, though there were others (e.g. from Ipswich to Norwich, Cromer etc.) which are not shown although Rackham no doubt used them.

INTRODUCTION

IN 1886 the publishers Carson and Comerford brought out a brilliantly evocative guide to the East Coast, written by Clement Scott, to which they gave the poetic title *Poppy-Land*. The book became an instant bestseller, and inspired thousands of holidaymakers to visit the Norfolk resort of Cromer, walk about the poppy-besprinkled cliffs in the vicinity, and then move on down the coast like Scott to explore Great Yarmouth, Lowestoft and other places in Suffolk.

For the first time in England's history these eastern counties, so long considered to be flat and uninteresting, were being properly valued as they ought to be for their exquisite scenery, fine old churches, noble manor houses and picturesque cottages. And they remained a favourite holiday destination for all classes of society right down to the First World War.

From 1886 to the 1920s *Poppy-Land* spawned a host of imitative books, magazine articles, songs and picture postcard series, to say nothing of thousands upon thousands of oil paintings and watercolours all entitled 'Poppyland.' Between 1886 and the end of the 1890s the whole of southern England was in fact gripped by rampant 'Scotto-mania.'

In order to cash in on this east coast fever, the large guide-book publishers Jarrold and Sons bought the rights to *Poppy-Land* in January 1893, and decided to bring out a new, illustrated fourth edition of the book in 1894. They commissioned a young artist, F. H. Townsend, whose sketches in *Punch*, the *Graphic* and the *Illustrated London News* they much admired, to go to the east coast and execute 26 pen and ink drawings of scenes mentioned in *Poppy-Land*.

In the spring of 1893 Jarrold and Sons also decided that when *Poppy-Land* made its refurbished appearance it should be accompanied by a sister book, a much more comprehensive guide, dealing with the whole of East Anglia, which they would call *Sunrise-Land*. They asked the popular writer Annie Berlyn, a close friend of Clement Scott, to undertake this project, and commissioned two more young artists, M. M. Blake and Arthur Rackham, to accompany her on her travels round the eastern counties, scheduled to take place between June 1893 and May 1894.

Born in London on 19th September 1867, the fourth of his parents' twelve children, Arthur Rackham was educated at the City of London School and Lambeth School of Art. In 1891 he began to contribute drawings to the *Pall Mall Budget*, and at New Year 1893 he left that paper and started to work for the *Westminster Budget* and *Westminster Gazette*.

In early 1893 Rackham made one or two mediocre drawings each for three works of fiction, and 20 sketches based on photographs for a guide book to America. But *Sunrise-Land* was his first major commission, for which he did over a hundred drawings (although in the event only 74 were actually used). And it was while leisurely touring East Anglia in 1893 and 1894 that he first really began to blossom as an illustrator, perfecting his purity of line and harmony of composition and working closely with the author.

It seems likely that Rackham owed this commission to Fred Townsend, his friend and fellow pupil at Lambeth School of Art. Townsend probably heard that Jarrold and Sons were looking for artists to illustrate *Sunrise-Land*, and recommended Arthur, who he knew would welcome some extra work. He may also have recommended Mr Blake, but unfortunately nothing can be discovered about this artist who is not mentioned in any reference book and did not attend Lambeth School of Art.

In whatever way it came about, however, there is no doubt that the *Sunrise-Land* commission was an extremely pleasant one, much enjoyed by Rackham. He had already spent a very agreeable summer holiday sightseeing in Norfolk with his family in 1881, and had gone yachting on the Norfolk Broads with his brother Harris in August 1892. So he knew Norfolk well and liked it, and was therefore only too happy to return to the county and then go on to explore the rest of East Anglia.

An unpublished caricature by Rackham, showing himself (right, in boater), his brother Harris (left), their friend William Ambrose and their yacht Young Rover, *from the visitors' book of the Horning Ferry inn.*

Both Arthur Rackham's travelling companions would have been congenial, too. Annie Berlyn was a charming, witty woman in her late twenties, who loved long walks as much as he himself did, and also shared to the full his fondness for picturesque buildings and stirring scenery. She had in addition a high regard for the French Impressionists, whom the artist greatly revered at that time. The pair must have got on well together, therefore. And we can see from the 67 drawings that M. M. Blake contributed to *Sunrise-Land* that although he sometimes produced mere hack work, his sketches were usually of a high standard and reveal a delicacy and sensitiveness that would have accorded well with the views of Rackham and Berlyn.

In 1893 and 1894 Mrs Berlyn and her party visited Norwich, Cromer, Wells-next-the-Sea, King's Lynn, Great Yarmouth, Lowestoft, Ipswich, Felixstowe, Aldeburgh, Southwold, Bury St Edmund's, Cambridge, Ely, Newmarket, Chelmsford, Harwich, Brightlingsea, Clacton, Southend Walton-on-the-Naze and Colchester. The three of them stayed for about a week in each town, always putting up at the best hotels, where they fared sumptuously off such delicacies as roast duck, Dover sole, oysters, asparagus and strawberries and cream. After sightseeing in the towns they toured the country round; sometimes on foot, sometimes in a hired carriage. Whenever occasion offered they also played tennis and golf and went fishing and boating.

Sometimes the trio took the train or a carriage straight from one centre to another, at others, as they were all Londoners with additional work to attend to, they returned to town for a while and then resumed their travels. They also often went back in winter to a place they had first visited in summer or autumn, so as to obtain a rounded view of the location.

The group's favourite hotel was the comfortable Crown Inn

Annie Berlyn and M. M. Blake in Holkham Park, drawn by Rackham in July 1893; published in Jarrold's Guide to Wells.

at Wells-next-the-Sea, where they spent a fortnight or so in July, 1893, being thoroughly spoilt by their landlady, 'the intelligent Mrs. Glazebrook', who apparently pandered to their every whim. In the evenings they played tennis in the back garden of the inn (picking strawberries, raspberries and currants between the sets), and during the day they went on excursions to such places as Holkham, Burnham Thorpe and Walsingham.

At Wells the party was joined by Lemmon Lingwood, one of Jarrolds' regular writers, who was preparing a guide to the district which was also due to come out in 1894. Arthur Rackham had been asked to supply 50 pen and ink drawings for this book, so, alternately accompanying Mrs Berlyn and Mr Lingwood, he must have had a busy time of it.

Twenty-five of Rackham's drawings for Jarrold's *Guide to Wells-next-the-Sea* depict the interior or exterior of churches or abbeys.

They are competent, workmanlike sketches, but possess little artistic merit. Of the remainder, one is of interest as demonstrating how the old village pump at Walsingham worked, another gives a fine view of East Barsham Manor House, three contain good tree studies and four are lively sketches of the quay at Wells. None of the drawings have the quality of the best illustrations in *Sunrise-Land*, however, and they are not worth reproducing.

As a change from hotels, for one week in June 1893 Annie Berlyn and the two artists stayed on a Fenland farm at 'sleepy Benwick'. Here they watched the sheep being sheared and the fields tended, and went on a trip to Peterborough, but otherwise spent most of their days 'leaning over the farm gate, looking across the dykes' at browsing cattle, turning windmills and barges sailing up and down the River Nene. Mrs Berlyn tells us that despite the fact that it is so flat, 'the artistically minded' cannot fail 'to find joy in Fenland'. Certainly she, Blake and Rackham seem to have had a delightful time there.

They also appear to have had a wonderful time when later that summer they hired a wherry on the Norfolk Broads for a week and sailed round Breydon Water, Horsey Mere, Hickling Broad, Barton Broad, Ranworth Broad, Irstead Broad, Rockland Broad and Wroxham Broad.

On sunny days the group often rowed off from the wherry in small boats and explored creeks and lakelets that larger craft could not enter, or went for walks in the surrounding woods or cornfields, always lunching at famous waterside inns such as the Swan at Horning. And when it rained they fished for eels, which 'furnished forth a dainty dish for the wherry dining table'.

The brief that Annie Berlyn, Arthur Rackham and M. M. Blake received from Jarrold and Sons seems to have been that they were to record just what took their fancy, not simply what was best known or most important in each place. As a result *Sunrise-Land* is a highly original guide book, full of unexpected snippets of information and drawings of unusual things. Mrs Berlyn gives a fascinating account of current Cambridge undergraduate life and customs, for example; she provides us with many intimate details about the royal family's daily routine at Sandringham; and she describes in depth the bizarre, virtually unknown village of Stiffkey, where the men did little work and the emancipated women spent their days cockling, dressed in the short divided skirts that Rackham has depicted so well.

Annie Berlyn was quick to note the 'characters' of all sorts that the three met on their travels, and encouraged Arthur to draw them, thus capturing for our delectation the pleasant old Walberswick ferryman, of whom the artists' colony there were very fond, the fantastically-dressed cockney couple on Southend beach and the wonderful, witch-like 'sisters' of Castle Rising almshouses, who provided the basic inspiration for all the bent old crones and witches that Rackham later drew to illustrate his fairy tales.

Castle Rising itself is an archetypal Norman castle with crumbling towers and turrets, mysterious doorways, long flights of stone steps. It not only caused Arthur to produce one of the most evocative sketches in *Sunrise-Land*, but also crops up again and again in his fairy-tale drawings and watercolours. This castle also probably kindled his interest in castles in general, especially those of Germany and Scandinavia which he visited in the late 1890s and early 1900s.

The two girls depicted in Arthur Rackham's drawing of Castle Rising are his sisters Meg and Winifred, who often posed for him in the 1890s. Winifred, his youngest sister, is the figure standing on the right. The two girls must have joined Arthur and his party on several jaunts during the summer holidays, for they feature again in their brother's sketch of the Abbey Gate at Bury St Edmund's, and also in Mr Blake's drawings of Overstrand and Harwich.

Rackham's sketches of his sisters demonstrate his keen observation of female fashions, a subject that occupied him all his life, and can clearly be seen in his drawings of seaside belles at Aldeburgh, Great Yarmouth, Lowestoft and Southend.

On these journeys to East Anglia Arthur was also able to enjoy to the utmost the depiction of water in all its manifestations: streams, rivers, ponds, lakes and the sea. This was another subject that remained dear to him all his life and reached its apotheosis with his illustrations to Izaak Walton's *The Compleat Angler,* published in 1931, several of which resemble the river scenes he drew at Bury St Edmund's and Chelmsford.

Trees, however, were always the things that Arthur Rackham liked drawing best, and his interest in their majestic forms and splendid silhouettes was shared by Annie Berlyn, who gave him every opportunity to indulge his preference to very good effect. For on these trips Rackham drew some of the most subtle tree studies he ever made.

All in all Rackham's journeys through the eastern counties in 1893 and 1894 provided him with a thorough apprenticeship in the art of pen and ink drawing. They also supplied him with a rich store of images which were to resurface again and again in his later artwork.

Jarrold's *Guide to Wells-next-the-Sea* by Lemmon Lingwood was published in the spring of 1894; *Sunrise-Land* and the new illustrated edition of *Poppy-Land* appeared some time in the summer of that year.

Sunrise-Land was issued simultaneously in a de-luxe 5*s* edition possessing a light mauve cover with an anonymous pastel drawing of the sun rising over the sea and a farmhouse and windmill on the shore, a 2*s* 6*d* edition with a grey cover and the same picture as the above, a second 2s 6*d* edition with a white cover embellished by a painting by W. A. Bettesworth showing a sailor sitting on a poppy-strewn cliff and gazing out to sea, and a paperback 1s edition which also has this painting on the cover.

Mr Lingwood's *Guide to Wells* could be obtained in hardback for 1s or paperback for 6*d*. Both versions have an evocative Bettesworth seascape with a tug in the foreground and two sailing ships in the background on the white cover. This edition, containing the 50 Rackham drawings, continued to be sold until about 1910, when Jarrolds produced new hardback and paperback guides to Wells written by W. R. Richmond. These contain only one of the Rackham sketches – the interior of Wells church – and possess an anonymous painting of Wells Quay on the cover.

Enlivened by Fred Townsend's spirited drawings, *Poppy-Land* became more popular than ever, new editions being called for almost every year until 1914. *Sunrise-Land* did not achieve quite the same renown, but it was a much loved, much respected book which went into four editions and remained in print until about 1908. Fellow travel writers such as H. V. Morton were still quoting from it, however, in the 1920s.

Some time in the late 1890s Jarrold and Sons published the first of their series of guides to Sheringham by Lemmon Lingwood, which continued to be sold until about 1905. All the known copies of this guide are undated, as many of Jarrolds' books were. But one early hardback edition contains Arthur Rackham's sketch of Bacton (wrongly captioned Cromer) from *Sunrise-Land*, an early paperback edition has Rackham's drawing of Holkham Hall from Jarrold's *Guide to Wells* and a small 32-page paperback edition of *c*. 1900 possesses four Rackham sketches from *Sunrise-Land*. All these versions have a white cover by Muriel Hannah, showing a woman reclining in a basket chair with a small bamboo table beside her.

In 1899 Jarrolds used seven of Arthur Rackham's drawings from *Sunrise-Land* to help illustrate William J. Tate's *East Coast Scenery*, a delightful collection of essays about seaside resorts and the countryside. This first and only edition of the book was on sale until about 1908 in two hardback versions, one having a pale green cover with photographs of Cambridge, Aldeburgh and Oulton Broad on it priced at 1*s* 6*d* and a 'superior' 3*s* 6*d* edition possessing an elegant blue and red cover with art nouveau flowers and leaves on it as well as a photograph of Ely Cathedral.

Jarrold and Sons also used 14 of Rackham's sketches from *Sunrise-Land* to adorn one of the most beautiful books they ever produced: Arthur Peaton's *Pictures of East Coast Health Resorts*, a most impressive quarto volume selling at 7*s* 6*d* and bound in red cloth with a design of poppies stamped on it in gold. This sole edition of the book came out in 1901 and remained in print down to 1910.

So far as can be ascertained at present there are no other books containing any of Arthur Rackham's East Anglian sketches, but new titles may come to light in the future. The artist always remained grateful to Jarrolds for having given him his first big assignment. And certainly the very varied drawing practice he obtained through the project stood him in good stead in his later career.

In 1900 Rackham won a modicum of recognition with his illustrations to Grimms' *Fairy Tales*. In 1905 he was greatly acclaimed for the watercolours he painted for Washington Irving's *Rip Van Winkle*. Finally in 1906 he shot to fame with his exquisite watercolours for J. M. Barrie's *Peter Pan in Kensington Gardens*.

Arthur Rackham never looked back but went from strength to strength right up to the time of his last commission, which was to illustrate Kenneth Grahame's *The Wind in the Willows*. This took him

Opposite: Great Eastern Railway fares list 1894.

GREAT EASTERN RAILWAY.

SEA-SIDE, & BROADS & RIVERS OF NORFOLK & SUFFOLK.

Tourist, Fortnightly, and Friday to Tuesday Tickets

ARE ISSUED AS UNDER BY ALL TRAINS :—

LIVERPOOL STREET OR ST. PANCRAS TO	Tourist.		Fortnightly.		Friday to Tuesday.	
	1 Class.	3 Class.	1 Class.	3 Class.	1 Class.	3 Class
Hunstanton	30/6	18/0	25/0	13/0	15/0	9/6
Lowestoft	33/0	19/9	27/6	15/0	20/0	10/0
Yarmouth	34/0	20/0	27/6	15/0	20/0	10/0
Cromer	34/0	20/0	27/6	15/0	20/0	10/0
Norwich	31/10	18/11	—	—	—	—
LIVERPOOL STREET TO						
Southend-on-Sea; Burnham-on-Crouch	8/8	4/4	7/0	4/4	6/0	3/6
Walton-on-the-Naze, Clacton-on-Sea, Frinton-on-Sea, Harwich, or Dovercourt	20/0	12/0	17/6	10/0	12/6	7/6
Felixstowe	23/4	14/3	17/6	10/0	12/6	7/6
Aldeburgh	27/9	16/9	25/0	13/0	15/0	9/6
Southwold	31/3	18/5	27/6	15/0	20/0	10/0

TOURIST TICKETS are issued daily from 1st May to the 31st of October, and are available for return any day up to and including the 31st of December of the year of issue.

FORTNIGHTLY TICKETS are issued daily, and are available for return any day within 15 days, including days of issue and return.

FRIDAY TO TUESDAY TICKETS are issued every Friday and Saturday, and are available for return on the day of issue, or on any day up to and including the following Tuesday.

TOURIST, FORTNIGHTLY, AND FRIDAY TO TUESDAY TICKETS to the above Stations are also issued from Great Eastern Stations within 12 miles of London at the same fares as from Liverpool Street. Passengers are allowed to travel to and from Liverpool Street to join or leave the fast Sea-Side Trains; also to and from Stratford to join or leave the Trains booked to call at that Station. They are also issued from New Cross (L. B. & S. C.) and all Stations on the East London Railway, at the same fares as Liverpool Street.

The above Tickets are available to and from additional Stations as follows:—*Southend-on-Sea Tickets* at Prittlewell; *Burnham-on-Crouch Tickets* at Southminster, *Clacton-on-Sea Tickets* at Frinton, Walton, Harwich, Dovercourt; *Walton-on-the-Naze Tickets* at Frinton, Clacton, Harwich, Dovercourt; *Frinton-on-Sea Tickets* at Clacton, Walton, Harwich, Dovercourt; *Harwich Tickets* at Dovercourt, Parkeston, Frinton, Clacton, Walton; *Felixstowe Tickets* at Trimley, Harwich; *Aldeburgh Tickets* at Leiston; *Southwold Tickets* at Darsham; *Hunstanton Tickets* at Heacham; *Lowestoft Tickets* at Beccles, Reedham, Carlton Colville, Oulton Broad Yarmouth, Cromer; *Yarmouth Tickets* at Beccles, Reedham, Acle, Lowestoft, Cromer; *Cromer Tickets* at Wroxham, North Walsham, Gunton, Yarmouth Lowestoft. Passengers must pay the ordinary local single fares when travelling from one Station to the other.

EXTRA JOURNEY RETURN TICKETS AT REDUCED FARES are issued at the above Stations, except Southend-on-Sea and Burnham-on-Crouch, to the Station from which the Tickets were issued, to holders of not less than two Tourist or Fortnightly Tickets.

EXTENSION OF TICKETS.—Passengers holding Friday to Tuesday Tickets and wishing to stay for a Fortnight or a shorter period, may do so by paying the difference between the Friday to Tuesday and Fortnightly Fares; and in the same manner Fortnightly Tickets may be extended to Tourist Tickets by paying the difference between those fares.

List of Farmhouse and County Lodgings in the Eastern Counties, and Pamphlets on the "Broads' District of Norfolk and Suffolk can be obtained (post free) on application to the Superintendent of the Line, Liverpool Street Station, London, E.C.

Liverpool Street Station, 1894. **WILLIAM BIRT,** *General Manager.*

from 1936 to 1939 and contains some of his finest work. Rackham died at his country house, Stilegate, Limpsfield, Surrey, on 6th September 1939.

The 40 pen and ink drawings from *Sunrise-Land* included in this book represent the best of Arthur Rackham's work for that publication. Unfortunately the actual drawings have been either lost or destroyed, although a few of the preliminary sketches for the finished drawings are in the Butler Library, Columbia University, New York. The drawings are so lucid, however, and Jarrolds printed them with such care, that the images in *Sunrise-Land* are exceedingly sharp and clear and reproduce well.

Rackham's method of working on the *Sunrise-Land* drawings appears to have been to make quick sketches of the scene before him in any location, and then to perfect these either when travelling in trains to a new place with Annie Berlyn and Mr Blake, or in hotels in the evenings. Each complete drawing as handed in to Jarrold and Sons measured 10 by 8 inches; in *Sunrise-Land* each drawing measures about 4 by 3 inches.

These drawings have hitherto been almost totally neglected by Arthur Rackham's biographers, but I hope that they will now gain the recognition that is their due for they not only deal with themes that the artist was later to develop so successfully in his children's book illustrations, but also provide us with fascinating glimpses of the vanished Victorian world with its horses and carts, gas lamps, village wells, sailing ships, bathing machines, boaters, sunbonnets and parasols.

ESSEX

*Chelmsford High Street
with the Shire Hall at the end,
which was built in 1792. The cows were
probably on their way to the Friday corn and cattle market.*

Tindal Square, Chelmsford, with the statue of Sir Nicholas Tindal (a native of the town), who was made Lord Chief Justice in 1829. The premises of the well known wine merchant Walter Gilbey, of Elsenham Hall, are at the back.

The 18th-century bridge over the River Can at Chelmsford.

River Can just outside Chelmsford.

The ruins of St Botolph's Priory, Colchester, built in 1100.

St John's Gateway in Stanway Street, Colchester, erected in the late 15th century.

Harwich harbour.

Women stripping seedpods at Carter and Co.'s seed and flower farm at St Osyth. This was the most famous flower farm in England at that time and attracted visitors from all over the country in summer.

A cockney Pearly King presenting his girlfriend with a a bottle of pickled cockles on Southend beach.

CAMBRIDGESHIRE

The Great Gate to Trinity College, Cambridge, built in 1535.

Fenland farm at Benwick, where Arthur Rackham, M. M. Blake and Annie Berlyn spent an idyllic week in June 1893.

SUFFOLK

Crag Path, Aldeburgh. The tower on the right is one of the watch towers belonging to the old 'beach companies', which, in the days before lifeboats, used them to watch for ships in difficulty during storms, and then put to sea to try and save both the ships and their occupants.

The Moot Hall, Aldeburgh, built in the early 16th century. The hall was once in the middle of the town, but is now on the beach, all the old houses round it having been swept away by the encroaching sea. To the left are the three famous Aldeburgh bathing machines.

The remains of Burgh Castle, an old Roman fort that was one of the strongholds belonging to the Count of the Saxon Shore.

The 12th-century Abbot's Bridge over the River Lark at Bury St Edmund's.

The Abbey Gate and garden, Bury St Edmund's, with Rackham's sister Meg seated on the bench and his sister Winifred holding a tennis racket. The Abbey was founded by King Canute in 1020.

The ruins of Leiston Abbey, built in 1389, as seen from the nearby farm.

The Fish Market, Lowestoft, where Annie Berlyn tells us smacks from all over Europe as well as England discharged their cargoes of 'plaice, soles, haddocks, mackerel and herrings'. Excellent whiting could be caught off the Fish Market quay.

The harbour basin, Lowestoft.

South Pier and Reading Rooms, Lowestoft, built in 1891. The pier was destroyed by bombs in the Second World War.

Pin Mill on the River Orwell.

An old well at Southwold.

Walberswick Ferry across the River Blyth.

NORFOLK

Bishop's Bridge, Norwich, built in 1249.

Guildhall and Market Place, Norwich. The Guildhall was mostly constructed between 1407 and 1413, but the Council Chamber was added in 1535. William Cobbett considered the market to be 'the best and most attractive' in England.

Pull's Ferry and the 15th-century Watergate, Norwich.

Tombland Alley, Norwich, one of the most picturesque parts of the city.

Tudor gateway to Baconsthorpe Hall.

Caister Castle, built in 1450 by Sir John Fastolf, on whom Shakespeare modelled his character Sir John Falstaff. The painter is M. M. Blake.

Stairway in the Norman Castle at Castle Rising, with Arthur Rackham's sisters Meg and Winifred in the foreground.

Two of the 'sisters' of Castle Rising almshouses, dressed in their Jacobean uniform of blue gowns, red cloaks and black, steeple-crowned hats, which made them look like fairy-tale witches.

Great Yarmouth beach.